HELLO GOD
ARE YOU HERE?

Written by
DONNA SMITH-HARPER

Copyright © 2023 Donna Smith-Harper.

Page Layout and Biblical Paraphrase by Mary Catherine Nelson

All rights reserved. No part of this book may be reproduced, stored, or transmitted by any means—whether auditory, graphic, mechanical, or electronic—without written permission of both publisher and author, except in the case of brief excerpts used in critical articles and reviews. Unauthorized reproduction of any part of this work is illegal and is punishable by law.

ISBN: 979-8-88640-887-4 (sc)
ISBN: 979-8-88640-888-1 (hc)
ISBN: 979-8-88640-889-8 (e)

Because of the dynamic nature of the Internet, any web addresses or links contained in this book may have changed since publication and may no longer be valid. The views expressed in this work are solely those of the author and do not necessarily reflect the views of the publisher, and the publisher hereby disclaims any responsibility for them.

One Galleria Blvd., Suite 1900, Metairie, LA 70001
1-888-421-2397

In Memory of James David Harper Jr.

Even unto them will I give in mine house and within my walls a place and a name better than of sons and of daughters: I will give them an everlasting name, that shall not be cut off. Isaiah 57:3 King James Version

Acknowledgements

A special thank you to Jason, Taylor, Owen, and Mordecai; not only for the inspiration you provide daily but also for the artwork which is included in Hello God. Thank you to Stephanie, Jason, Scott, and Melissa. You all have talents that you willingly share! Without you, this book would not have become a reality.

Borrowing words from Mordecai and Stephanie, I'd like to say, "Hello God, thank you for whispering to me and giving me words to write."

Hello, God. Are you here?

My mommy says You are, but I never saw You before. If You are really here, please show me. My friends can't come out to play in the rain. I really want to play today.

So . . . if You are here . . . Please God . . . come out, come out, where ever You are! I am ready to play!

I searched high and low. Upstairs in my bedroom and down under the sofa; You were nowhere to be found. Mommy said that You are always with me.

Usually she is very reliable. Don't know if I should believe her. I am not sure because I have never seen You. She said You were my friend. Are You real or are You my imaginary friend? Come on, let's play!

Don't be scared. I promise not to bite.

Me and my friend, Hunter, were playing in the yard yesterday. We looked all over for You. We wanted to play "Hide and Seek" with You.

If Mommy is right about You . . . . Well, I am wondering, God, where were you hiding? By the way, God, You hide really good. Mommy says I have to take turns when I play with my friends. We should take turns playing "Hide and Seek." Let me hide just one time, then You can find me!

Mommy took me and my sister to the park. She said You were with us when that man in the big red monster truck almost hit our car.

I didn't see You in our car. I thought You might be riding on top so you could feel the wind blowing. You KNOW how I like to feel the wind in my hair. When I got out of the car, You were nowhere to be found. Where were You hiding?

Mommy says You are in my heart. Is that right? How did You get in there?!

Sometimes Daddy takes me kite flying. I am really, really good at flying a kite. Daddy said I could not fly my kite if You did not make the wind blow.

I don't know how You made the wind blow, but I am so glad You did it. Do You think You could show me how so I can make the wind blow too?

I really like when Mommy lets me go down the slide by myself! I go so fast I can feel the breeze in my hair!! And, it feels just like someone is hugging me!!! It was not my Mommy hugging me because she was waiting at the bottom to catch me. Was it You holding me as we flew down the slide?

So how did You get into my heart?

I want to get to KNOW You. I think I'd like to be Your friend.

Mommy and Daddy and I went to the beach. You should have been there, God!

We had so much fun splashing in the waves and building sand castles, and, oh yeah, we found some seashells on the beach! Mommy said that You made the waves using the same wind that made my kite fly. She also said that You left the seashells in the sand for me to find! Thank You, God. Mommy said You painted the ocean and the sky too! I sure didn't know You could design a project like that! I like to paint too. Do You think we could design something really cool together?

Mommy makes me wear a smock so I won't mess up my clothes. "Smock" is just a fancy word for an apron for artists. I bet you don't have to wear a smock. Mommy and Daddy agree with our preacher; You never make mistakes.

Really, I want to know. How did You get into my heart? I really want to be Your friend. It's okay for You to tell me how it happened. Friends do that, You know? They talk to each other.

Daddy is my friend. Sometimes we play ball together. You know Gracie. She is my baby sister. Well, she is too little to play ball. I really like it when my daddy plays ball with me. Just me and Daddy, like before Gracie came to live with us. Did she live with you before then?

One day I heard Daddy say that You were his Father. I really do not understand that. God, are You my granddaddy?

Daddy took me and Mommy and Gracie to the lake and we went fishing there. You should have seen it, God! That lake was huge!

Mommy was scared to put bait on the hook, but not me. Daddy and me, we were brave! He taught me how to bait my hook exactly the same way Granddaddy taught him to bait his hook. We baited Mommy's hook for her.

Girls are afraid of way too many things. Daddy said us boys have to take care of our girls. But I don't mind because I know my Mommy takes care of me bunches; more than I take care of her.

My daddy is a fish catching machine. He caught five fishes! Mommy caught a little fish. Daddy said the fish would taste really good for supper. That's what we call our meal that we eat at night, supper!

Guess what! I caught the biggest fish! Thought that I had a shark on my hook! Daddy said that it could not be a shark because sharks swim in the ocean not in the lake. And there we were at the lake catching fish.

It seemed like it took forever, but I finally got that big fish on land! Daddy said it was a bass. My fish was not very big. Boy! That little bass put up a good fight!

And You know what, God? Yep, that's right! We ate fish for supper! My daddy knows everything. He said that the fish would taste good . . . and it did. My tummy was so full of fish.

My daddy knows You, God! He said that You are a fisher man too. I asked Daddy how he knew You. He said, he believed in You, and You came into his heart. All he had to do was invite You into his heart.

Did he send You an invitation in the mail like I do for my birthday party? Is that how You got into my heart? Do You love me too?

Daddy said that You were his Father, and Mommy's Father, and my Father, and Gracie's Father too. I don't understand how that can be. Daddy said that I will understand when I am a little older. He told me I need to believe what he says and trust and obey. Obey, that's a big word for mind, isn't it? Sometimes I get in trouble for not minding. Am I getting in trouble for not obeying?

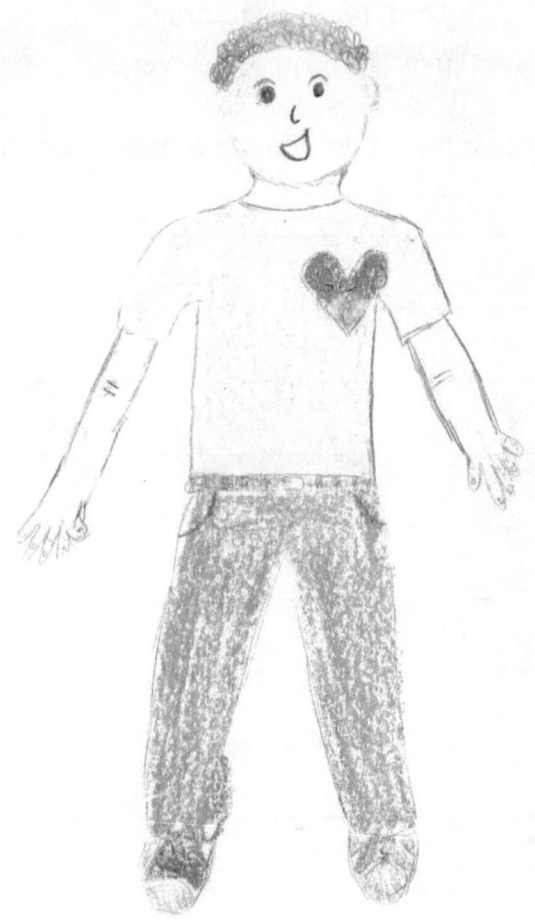

Daddy said I will understand soon all about You, God. And, then he said something about God's time. Do you have a special watch like a super hero?

I live in the Eastern Time zone, God. Do You live in the Mountain Time zone? I heard that You could be found high up on a mountain. How can that be?

You are in my heart like Mommy said! You are! You are too in my heart! You are my friend!

Lord, teach us to pray . . . .
Luke 11:1 King James Version

You may write a few of your favorite prayers on this page.

www.ingramcontent.com/pod-product-compliance
Lightning Source LLC
LaVergne TN
LVHW042157070526
838201LV00047BA/1559